KAZU KIBUISHI

BOOK ONE
THE STONEKEEPER

AN IMPRINT OF

📖 SCHOLASTIC

NEW YORK TORONTO LONDON AUCKLAND SYDNEY MEXICO CITY NEW DELHI HONG KONG BUENOS AIRES

Library of Congress Cataloging-in-Publication Data is available.

ISBN-978-93-89823-91-2

First edition, January 2008
This edition: November 2022

Edited by Sheila Keenan
Creative Director: David Saylor
Book Design by Phil Falco

Printed in India

PROLOGUE

WE HAVE PLENTY OF TIME—

AT LEAST HALF AN HOUR.

WE'RE SUPPOSED TO PICK UP NAVIN AT EIGHT O'CLOCK.

WE'RE LATE.

FIFTEEN MINUTES IS NOT A HALF HOUR.

I THINK DAD JUST LIVES IN AN ALTERNATE UNIVERSE.

TIME MOVES SLOWER THERE.

THAT CERTAINLY WOULD EXPLAIN A FEW THINGS.

I'M SURE NAVIN WON'T MIND PLAYING VIDEO GAMES FOR A FEW MINUTES LONGER, HONEY.

HEY DAD, I GET TO PLAY A GAME WHEN WE GET THERE, RIGHT?

MM-HMM.

SIT BACK DOWN, EMILY.

OKAY, COOL.

DAVID, IT'S ALREADY LATE. BY THE TIME WE GET BACK HOME, IT'LL BE PAST ELEVEN.

YOU'RE RIGHT. YOU'RE RIGHT.

HEAR THAT, EMILY? WE'LL HAVE TO POSTPONE OUR GAME TILL NEXT TIME.

AWW.

DAVID—

4

WHUD!

EMILY, I CAN'T. MY LEGS ARE STUCK UNDER THE DASHBOARD.

KRRRKK...

DAD, JUST GIVE ME YOUR HAND. PLEASE.

EMILY— YOU'LL NEED HELP...

MOM! DAD'S STUCK!!

DAVID?! YOU HAVE TO GET OUT OF THERE RIGHT NOW!

KAREN, MY LEGS ARE STUCK.

WE NEED SOMEONE TO PRY ME OUT OF HERE...GET HELP.

DAVID, WE DON'T HAVE TIME!!

KRRRRK!

THE CAR'S TIPPING!!

JUST GIVE ME YOUR HAND!!!

10

BOOK ONE
THE STONEKEEPER

2 YEARS LATER

IF YOU KEEP THAT UP, YOUR FACE WILL STAY THAT WAY.

JUST SO LONG AS YOU BOTH FIND SOME WAY TO BE ENTERTAINED AND STAY OUT OF TROUBLE,

I DON'T CARE WHAT YOU DO WITH YOUR FACES.

I'M TRYING TO CHEER UP EM.

SHE'S MAKING THE MOPEY FACE AGAIN.

HEY!

DON'T LISTEN TO HIM, MOM. I'M DOING FINE.

ANYWAY, I THINK YOU GUYS WILL LIKE THIS TOWN. THEY HAVE MINIATURE GOLF.

THE ONLY CATCH IS THAT THIS HOUSE WILL REQUIRE A LOT OF WORK TO MAKE IT COMFORTABLE.

WHY DID WE LEAVE OUR OTHER PLACE? EVERYTHING THERE WAS BRAND NEW.

UNFORTUNATELY, NEW THINGS COST A LOT. SINCE YOUR FATHER PASSED AWAY, I HAVEN'T BEEN ABLE TO AFFORD THAT HOUSE,

AT LEAST OUT HERE, WE WON'T BE UNDER QUITE AS MUCH FINANCIAL STRAIN. THIS HOUSE HAS BEEN IN THE FAMILY FOR YEARS.

MOM, WE'RE OUT IN THE MIDDLE OF NOWHERE.

THERE ARE PLENTY OF PLACES IN THIS COUNTRY THAT ARE OUT IN "THE MIDDLE OF NOWHERE" --

NONE OF WHICH ARE QUITE AS POPULOUS AS NORLEN. IT'S A FAIRLY SIZABLE CITY.

NOW ENTERING NORLEN POP. 28,000

YOU'LL SEE. IT'S NOT THAT DIFFERENT THAN ANYWHERE ELSE.

WELL, HERE WE ARE.

THIS HOME IS GOING TO REQUIRE **A LOT** OF LOVE.

EVERYONE STAY CLOSE.

WATCH YOUR STEP.

THERE'S SIMPLY NO WAY WE CAN SLEEP HERE UNDER THESE CONDITIONS.

Sigh.

...WE'LL HAVE TO ATTACK IT.

SHHFF

BDUMP

FSSHK!

21

SILAS CHARNON

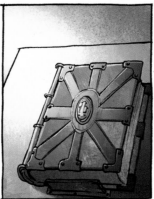

On Stone Power

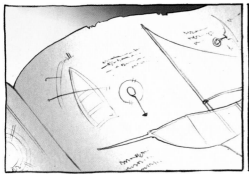

EMILY!

EMILY?

WHOA.

DISAPPEARED?

NAVIN!

AFTER YOUR GREAT GRANDMOTHER ISABEL PASSED AWAY, SILAS LOCKED HIMSELF IN THIS HOUSE AND WAS NEVER SEEN AGAIN.

THIS IS WHY THE LOCALS THINK THIS PLACE IS **HAUNTED**.

IS IT?

OF COURSE NOT.

GET DOWN FROM THERE!

C'MON, MOM!

I'LL BE ALL RIGHT!

THERE'S NOTHING UP HERE BUT OLD JUNK!

THERE ARE SO MANY BLUEPRINTS. WAS HE AN ARCHITECT?

NO.

SILAS WAS A PUZZLE MAKER. I KNOW HE WAS PROUD OF THAT FACT.

ALTHOUGH, I ALWAYS THOUGHT HIS PUZZLES LOOKED MORE LIKE TOYS OR MACHINES.

CARDBOT

WOW.

YOU SAID GREAT GRANDPA DIDN'T GO TO SCHOOL, RIGHT?

AND LOOK AT ALL THE COOL STUFF HE DID.

EMILY—

MY GRANDFATHER WAS ECCENTRIC.

AND HE'S NOT SOMEONE YOU SHOULD LOOK UP TO.

WHY NOT?

JUST TRUST ME, EMILY. IT'S BETTER TO LEAD A NORMAL LIFE, LIKE EVERYONE ELSE.

NOW LET'S GO DOWNSTAIRS AND FINISH CLEANING.

WE HAVE A LOT TO DO BEFORE IT GETS DARK.

SSSHF

I WOULDN'T DO THAT IF I WERE YOU.

WHY NOT?

BECAUSE IT'S CREEPY.

OH, GROW UP.

SHK!

OW!

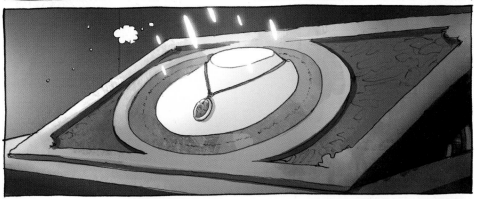

C'MON EM, WE SHOULD LEAVE IT ALONE AND TELL MOM ABOUT IT.

SHE'LL JUST TELL US TO PUT IT BACK.

HERE, HELP ME PUT IT ON.

I'M NOT GOOD AT TYING KNOTS.

IT'S EASY. JUST MAKE TWO PRETZELS.

TWO
PRETZELS.

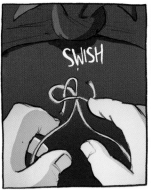
SWISH

SHK!

DID YOU
TIE IT?

I, UM—
I THINK
SO.

IT'S
BEAUTIFUL.

DON'T TELL
MOM, OKAY?

I WANT
ONE,
TOO.

I'LL LET YOU
WEAR IT WHEN
I'M DONE
WITH IT.

C'MON.

LET'S GO
HELP MOM.

CLICK!

THE POWER SHOULD COME BACK ON IN A COUPLE OF DAYS.

UNTIL THEN, IT'LL BE LIKE WE'RE OUT CAMPING.

WHAT'S WRONG EMILY?

WHY DID WE MOVE OUT HERE?

HONESTLY.

I THOUGHT YOU GUYS WOULD LIKE ALL THIS NATURE.

YOU ALWAYS LOVED SUMMER CAMP.

YEAH, BUT WE ONLY DO THAT FOR A MONTH OUT OF THE YEAR.

NOT, LIKE, FOREVER.

LOOK, I JUST WANTED FOR US TO START A NEW LIFE AND LEAVE THE OLD ONE BEHIND.

I WANTED TO START FRESH. THERE'S NOTHING WRONG WITH THAT, RIGHT?

BUT WE DIDN'T HAVE TO COME ALL THE WAY OUT HERE TO DO THAT.

IT'S NOT SOMETHING DAD WOULD HAVE DONE.

GULP.

WHY DO YOU SAY THINGS LIKE THAT, EMILY?

BUT IT'S THE TRUTH.

LOOK, I JUST—

I DON'T—

I LOVE YOU BOTH SO MUCH.

I DON'T KNOW WHAT I WOULD DO IF I LOST YOU, TOO.

YOU WON'T.

ZZZZZ

HOW ARE YOU DOING, EMILY?

ARE YOU WARM?

I'M GOOD. THANKS MOM.

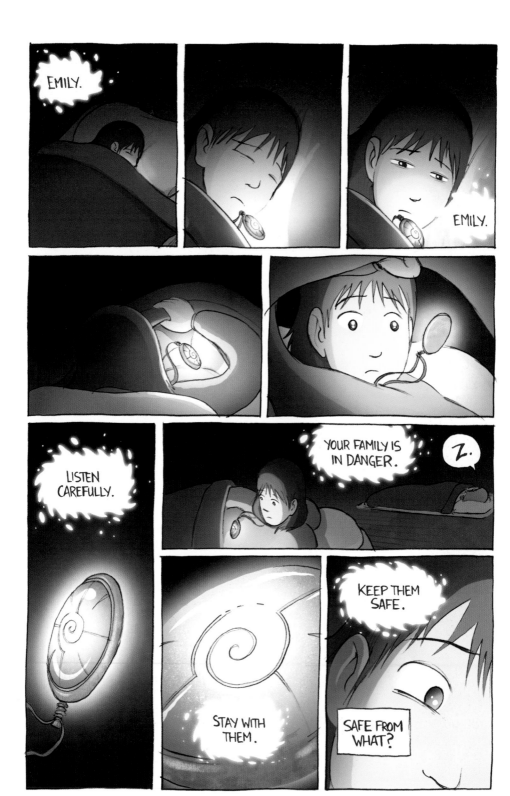

WAIT!

K-THUMP!!

K-THUMP!!

YOU HEAR THAT?

IT'S COMING FROM DOWN-STAIRS.

MOM, WHAT IS THAT?

K-THUMP!

I DON'T KNOW, NAVIN.

CLICK!

YOU TWO STAY HERE WHILE I GO SEE WHAT IT IS.

WE'LL GO WITH YOU.

STAY CLOSE.

K-THUMP!

HELLO?!

IT'S PROBABLY JUST THE PIPES.

OR MAYBE A RACCOON.

RACCOON?

SOUNDS LIKE IT'S COMING FROM THE BASEMENT.

K-THUMP!

KRRRK..

I WANT YOU BOTH TO STAY HERE WHERE IT'S SAFE.

IF IT'S REALLY AN ANIMAL, I DON'T WANT YOU GETTING NEAR IT.

IT MAY BITE.

I WANT TO GO WITH YOU.

NO. YOU STAY HERE.

LOCK THIS DOOR IF I SAY SO, OKAY?

MOMMM.

DO AS I SAY!

I'LL BE BACK QUICKLY.

I PROMISE.

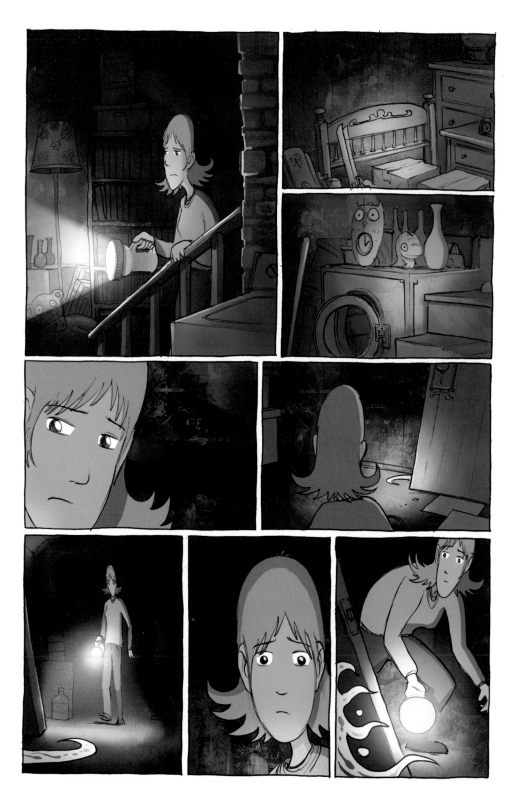

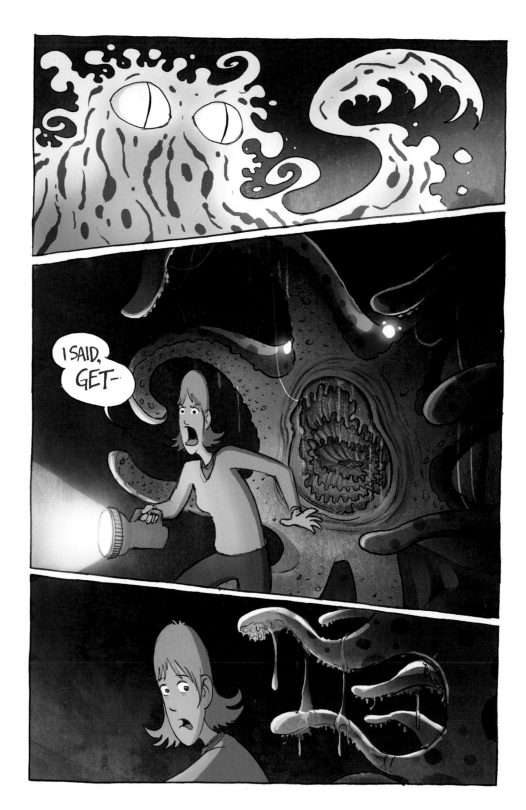

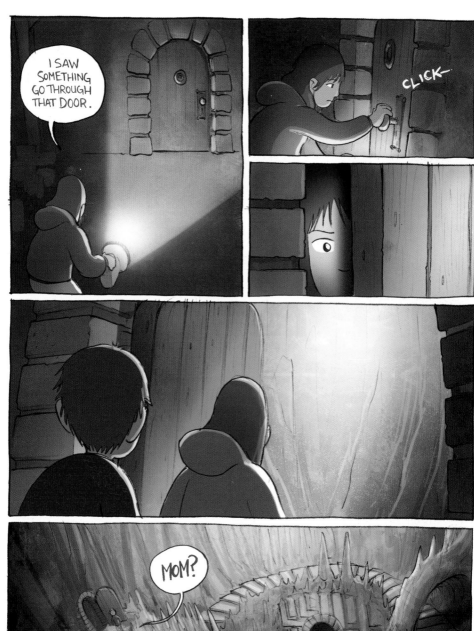

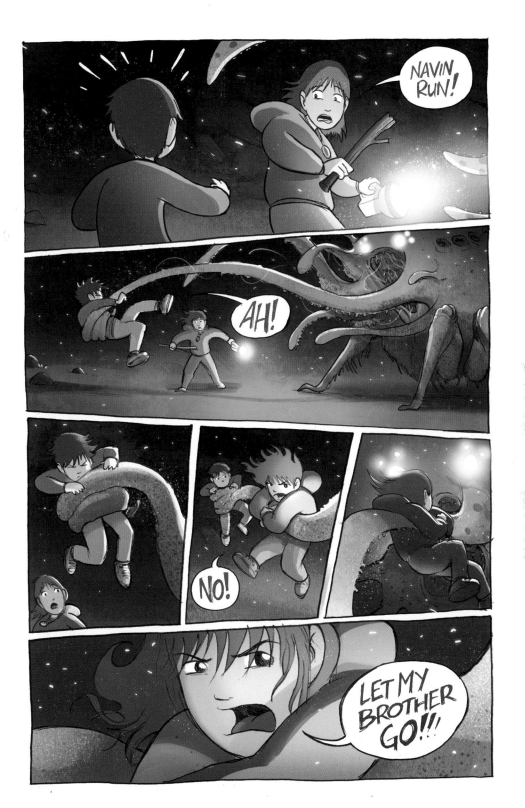

SKREEEE!

EM!

NAVIN!

ERGH!

GAH!

SKREE!

C'MON! GET UP!!!

GO TOWARD THE ROCKS!

SNAP!

?

GRUNT GRUNT

IS IT GONE?

IT'S STILL CLOSE.

WHAT DO WE DO ABOUT MOM?

I DON'T KNOW.

EMILY.

IF YOU WANT TO SAVE YOUR MOTHER, LISTEN VERY CAREFULLY.

MAKE YOUR WAY DOWN INTO THE RAVINE AND FIND THE CAVERN'S CREEK.

FOLLOW IT UPSTREAM TO THE WATER'S SOURCE...

AND THERE YOU WILL FIND A HOUSE BUILT ON A COLUMN OF ROCK.

BEWARE THE CREATURES WHO STAND IN YOUR WAY.

WHATEVER HAPPENS, YOU MUST SEEK THE AID OF THE MAN WHO LIVES AT THE HOUSE...

YOUR GREAT GRANDFATHER, SILAS CHARNON.

IT'S A DEAD END.

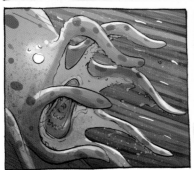

THE UMBRELLA MUSHROOMS.

PULL THEM OUT BY THE ROOTS AND USE THEM AS SAILS.

SAILS?

YOU OKAY?

YEAH.

HEY EM, IF YOU LEAN YOU CAN STEER IT.

TRY TO KEEP IT STEADY.

BOOMP!

HUH?

PECK!
PECK!

EM!
SOMETHING'S EATING MY PARACHUTE!

PECK! PECK!

JUST HOLD ON!

I'M COMING! HOLD TIGHT!

PECK! PECK!

KICK!
SQUAWK!

SQUAWK!
KICK! KICK! KICK!!

PECK! PECK!

I'LL COME BACK AROUND, NAVIN.

HWEEEEE

IN ABOUT ONE MINUTE, THAT CONEBEAK WILL MAKE ITS WAY THROUGH THE CAP.

WHEN THAT HAPPENS, NAVIN WILL FALL TO HIS DEATH.

WHAT CAN I DO?!

USE THE AMULET.

HWEEEE

PECK. PECK. PECK.

YOU'VE DONE IT ALREADY.

YOU CAN DO IT AGAIN.

NO MORE FEAR.

JUST FOCUS...

AND PROJECT THAT ENERGY...

VRRRRN

WAIT,
I MEAN
A WITCH.
YOU'RE A
WITCH.

STOP IT,
NAVIN.
I'M NOT
A WITCH.

BUT THAT
WAS SO
MAGICAL.

KSSSH!

NOW REMEMBER
TO USE THIS
POWER WISELY.

BEING A STONEKEEPER
IS A RESPONSIBILITY
YOU MUSTN'T TAKE
LIGHTLY.

A STONEKEEPER?

WHAT DO WE DO ABOUT MOM?

TRICKLE TRICKLE

HOW DO YOU KNOW WE CAN TRUST IT?

THAT VOICE SOUNDED PRETTY SHIFTY.

TRICKLE TRICKLE

THE AMULET SAID TO GO UPSTREAM AND FOLLOW THE WATER TO ITS SOURCE.

WE BETTER DO AS IT SAYS.

THAT SHIFTY VOICE SAVED YOUR LIFE.

AND IT'S NOT LIKE WE'VE GOT A LOT OF OPTIONS, NAVIN.

SO UNLESS YOU COME UP WITH A BETTER PLAN,

THE AMULET WILL BE OUR GUIDE.

EMILY.

DON'T LET NAVIN OUT OF YOUR SIGHT.

HUH?

NAVIN!

NAVIN! GET AWAY FROM THOSE THINGS!!

THEY'RE HARMLESS, EM.

HOW DO YOU KNOW THEY'RE NOT DISEASED?!

C'MON, GET UP.

I CAN'T HAVE YOU GETTING SICK OR HURT NOW.

75

THAT MUST BE THE HOUSE.

WE'LL HAVE TO CROSS.

YOU READY TO SWIM?

NAVIN?

SOMEBODY'S COMING.

SHK!
!

HUMMMM

WHAT IS THAT?

HOLD STILL, AND DON'T SAY A WORD.

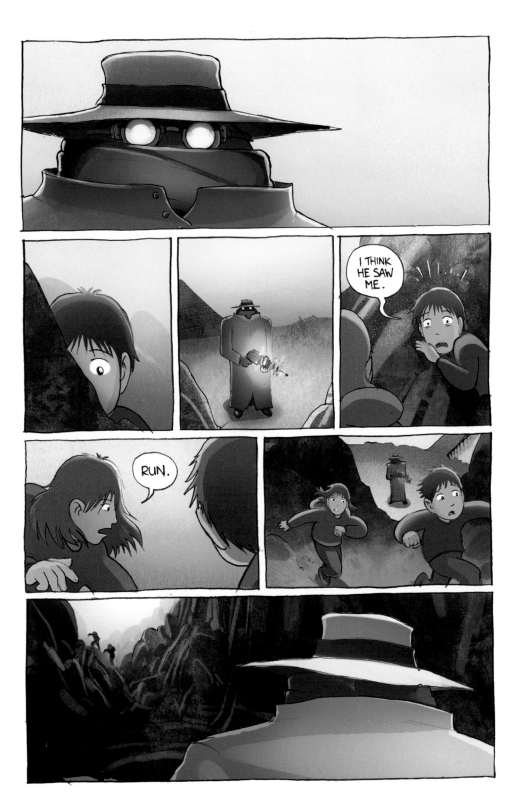

VRRRN

VAK!

SKSHHHH

YOU KILLED HIM!

I ONLY STUNNED HIM.

HE'LL GET UP SOON, SO WE MUST HURRY.

HUMMMMM

TO THE BOAT.

QUICKLY.

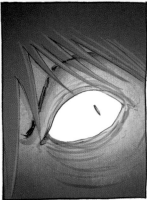

HE'S COMING BACK!

HOLD ON TIGHT.

86

WHAT DOES HE WANT FROM US?

THE AMULET.

LIKE MANY OTHERS, HE SEEKS ITS POWER.

AND HOW DO I KNOW YOU'RE NOT AFTER IT AS WELL?

BECAUSE I'M THE ONE WHO HELPED GET IT TO YOU.

IT IS A GIFT FROM YOUR GREAT GRANDFATHER, SILAS CHARNON.

HE HAS CHOSEN YOU TO INHERIT THE AMULET'S POWER.

AND WHO ARE YOU?

I AM HIS ASSISTANT.

WILL SILAS BE ABLE TO HELP US GET OUR MOM BACK?

YOU WILL HAVE THE OPPORTUNITY TO ASK HIM YOURSELF.

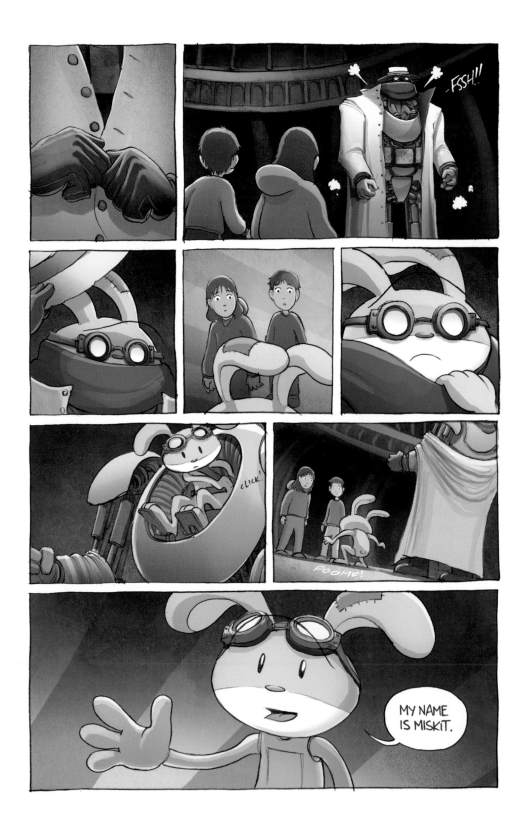

UM, HELLO.

SHAKE

NOW PLEASE FOLLOW ME.

IT'S AN HONOR TO MEET YOU, EMILY.

EVERYONE IS WAITING.

EVERYONE?

WHO'S EVERYONE?

HERE THEY COME, RUBY.

SQUEET.

YOU'RE KIDDING, RIGHT?

THEY'RE JUST A COUPLA RUNTS!

HAVE SOME RESPECT, COGSLEY. SILAS KNOWS WHAT HE'S DOING.

I HOPE YOU'RE RIGHT.

DON'T MIND HIM.

HE'S ALWAYS LIKE THAT.

OH, THANK GOODNESS YOU'RE HERE.

WHAT'S THE MATTER?

TAKE A LOOK AT HIS READINGS.

THEY'RE GROWING WEAKER.

HE EVEN FAINTED EARLIER, WHEN I TRIED TO FEED HIM.

IF THIS KEEPS UP--

OH, THESE MUST BE THE CHILDREN.

IT'S A PLEASURE TO MEET YOU.

MY NAME IS MORRIE.

I'M EMILY, AND THIS IS NAVIN.

A PLEASURE.

PSSSH

SIR... THEY'RE HERE.

THEY MADE IT.

YOU'RE SILAS CHARNON?

YES, MY DEAR. AND YOU MUST BE MISS EMILY HAYES.

AND THIS MUST BE MASTER NAVIN.

DID YOU BUILD ALL THIS STUFF?

YES.

WITH THE HELP OF A FEW FRIENDS, OF COURSE.

SO YOU KNOW WHY WE'RE HERE.

YES.

OUR MOTHER IS IN DANGER.

THE AMULET TOLD US TO FIND YOU, AND THAT YOU WOULD HELP US.

CAN YOU HELP US?

BUT MY DEAR, YOU MUST UNDERSTAND--

--THAT I ALREADY HAVE.

HWEEEEE

LET ME TELL YOU A LITTLE ABOUT YOUR INHERITANCE.

THE AMULET CONTAINS A STONE THAT CAN GRANT SOMEONE THE POWER TO RULE THE LAND OF ALLEDIA.

ALLEDIA?

IT IS WHERE YOU ARE NOW, AN ALTERNATE VERSION OF OUR PLANET EARTH.

IN TIME, YOU WILL KNOW THE LAND AND ITS PEOPLE.

YOU WILL SEE HOW BEAUTIFUL IT IS.

BUT WHAT DOES THIS HAVE TO DO WITH HELPING US?

THAT WILL BECOME EVIDENT WHEN YOU REALIZE THE EXTENT OF THE STONE'S ABILITIES.

IF YOU CAN MASTER IT,

YOU WILL NOT ONLY SAVE YOUR MOTHER'S LIFE,

BUT YOU WILL GAIN A GREAT AND GLORIOUS POWER BEYOND ANYTHING YOU EVER IMAGINED.

IT IS SOMETHING I FAILED TO ATTAIN DURING MY LIFETIME.

BUT YOU... YOU CAN ACHIEVE IT.

BUT I'M NOT INTERESTED IN POWER.

I JUST WANT TO GET MY MOM BACK AND GO HOME.

BUT WHAT IF I TOLD YOU THIS POWER WOULD ALLOW YOU TO **TURN BACK TIME?** TO MAKE THINGS GO BACK TO THE WAY THEY ONCE WERE?

THERE MUST HAVE BEEN A TIME IN YOUR LIFE WHEN YOU WERE HAPPIER.

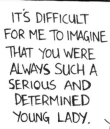

IT'S DIFFICULT FOR ME TO IMAGINE THAT YOU WERE ALWAYS SUCH A SERIOUS AND DETERMINED YOUNG LADY.

YOU CAN HAVE WHAT YOU'RE REALLY LOOKING FOR...

AND ALL YOU HAVE TO DO IS LISTEN TO THE STONE.

IT WILL HELP YOU ATTAIN THE POWER TO SHAPE YOUR WORLD.

IT WILL GIVE YOU EVERYTHING YOU DESIRE, AND MUCH MORE.

I ONLY WISH I COULD BE THERE TO SHARE IT WITH YOU.

EMILY, WHEN I AM GONE, YOU WILL BE LEFT WITH A CHOICE.

YOU MAY CHOOSE TO ACCEPT THE STONE'S POWER OR TO TURN IT AWAY.

JUST REMEMBER THAT EITHER CHOICE COMES WITH GREAT CONSEQUENCES AND SACRIFICE.

BUT WHY? WHY ME?

BECAUSE I KNOW YOU WON'T LET ME DOWN.

MISKIT.

YES SIR.

I LEFT ALL OF MY THOUGHTS AND MEMORIES IN YOUR DATABANKS.

IT WILL BE YOUR JOB TO TEACH EMILY AND LEAD HER DOWN THE RIGHT PATH.

YOU WERE MY APPRENTICE, AND NOW EMILY WILL BE YOURS.

BUT SIR, I'M NOT READY.

YOU WERE BORN READY!

THIS IS WHAT I BUILT YOU FOR.

BUT SIR, I CAN'T DO THIS ON MY OWN.

BUT YOU'RE NOT ALONE.

SO CALM YOURSELF. YOUR FEARS ARE UNWARRANTED.

THE MOMENT I SAW THEIR FACES, I KNEW EVERYTHING WAS GOING TO BE ALL RIGHT.

THAT'S THE FEELING I'VE BEEN WAITING FOR MY ENTIRE LIFE.

YOU CAN'T JUST LEAVE US WITH A COUPLE OF KIDS!

IS... IS HE DEAD?

SILAS...

DON'T LEAVE US...

WHIRRRRRR

WHIRRR CLICK!

?

WHY ARE YOU LOOKING AT ME LIKE THAT?

WHIRRRR CLICK! WHIRRRR CLICK!

WITH SILAS GONE, YOU'RE OUR ONLY HOPE.

PLEASE DON'T TURN AWAY!

IT IS TIME TO CHOOSE.

TAKE SILAS'S PLACE AS KEEPER OF THIS STONE...

AND YOU WILL AWAKEN A FAMILY THAT CAN HELP YOU RECOVER YOUR OWN.

JUST TAKE THE AMULET INTO YOUR HANDS AND ACCEPT ITS POWER.

EM, WAIT.

I DON'T TRUST IT.

WITHOUT POWER YOU CANNOT ATTAIN WHAT YOU DESIRE.

EM,
DON'T
DO IT.

WITHOUT THE
STONE, ALL THAT
SURROUNDS YOU
WILL TURN TO
DUST.

EMBRACE
THE POWER...

AND USE IT
TO SAVE YOUR
FAMILY.

NAVIN,
WE NEED THEIR
HELP.

HEY!! WE'RE ALIVE! WE'RE STILL IN BUSINESS!

OH, THANK SILAS! THAT WAS CLOSE.

WE'LL TAKE IT FROM HERE, SIR.

SNAP!

KRRRK!

SHWEEE

SHWEEE

THEODORE, PUT SILAS IN A SLEEP CHAMBER AND PREPARE HIM FOR TRANSPORT TO KANALIS.

YES SIR.

SHWEEE

WE'LL HAVE TO CONSULT THE MAIN COMPUTER TO LOCATE YOUR MOTHER.

PLEASE FOLLOW ME.

EM, I GET THE FEELING YOU'RE GETTING US IN DEEPER AND DEEPER TROUBLE.

LISTEN, WITHOUT MOM HERE, I'M THE ONE IN CHARGE, OKAY?

I CAN HANDLE THIS.

THIS IS A MAP OF OUR CURRENT LOCATION: GONDOA MOUNTAIN.

THE MAP ALSO SHOWS US ALL OF THE LIFE FORMS MOVING WITHIN THE SPACE.

THERE.

THAT'S THE CREATURE CARRYING YOUR MOTHER.

IT'S HEADING NORTH TOWARD MORLEY'S CAVE.

IF--

SAY IT AIN'T SO, CHIEF!

DON'T TELL ME WE'RE WORKING FOR THESE MUNCHKINS NOW.

EMILY IS NOW OUR CAPTAIN.

SHE'S JUST A KID!

THIS WAS SILAS'S LAST ORDER.

HMPH.

MISKIT, YOU SAID SHE WAS HEADING UP TO MORLEY'S CAVE, RIGHT?

RIGHT.

WELL, THERE'S A TUNNEL THAT COULD TAKE US RIGHT THERE.

WE CAN HEAD THEM OFF BEFORE THEY LEAVE THE CAVE.

THAT'S NOT JUST ANY TUNNEL, KID.

THAT'S THE GAUNTLET!

SEE THOSE LIFE FORMS ALONG THE WALLS?

THOSE ARE RAKERS.

WHAT ARE RAKERS?

RAKERS ARE SOME OF THE MOST FEROCIOUS UNDERGROUND DWELLERS ON ALLEDIA.

THEY'RE BASICALLY LARGE MASSES OF TENTACLES AND TEETH, EATING ANYTHING THAT THEY CAN GET AHOLD OF.

TRAVELING THROUGH THERE ON FOOT CAN MEAN CERTAIN DEATH.

WHAT OTHER OPTIONS DO WE HAVE?

THE ALBATROSS.

YOU CAN TAKE THE ALBATROSS THROUGH THE GAUNTLET.

BUT THAT JALOPY HASN'T FLOWN IN YEARS!

YOU JUST GET PREPARED FOR TAKEOFF.

I'LL WORRY ABOUT GETTING IT RUNNING.

CAN WE TRUST HIM?

COGSLEY CAN BE A REAL PAIN IN THE BUTT,

BUT HE'S ALSO THE MOST HONEST, HARD-WORKING ROBOT I KNOW.

IT LOOKS LIKE I ONLY HAVE TWO TRANQUILIZER DARTS.

WE'LL HAVE TO MAKE EVERY SHOT COUNT.

WHAT DO WE DO AFTER IT'S SEDATED?

WE HARPOON IT AND THEN WE DRAG IT TO A STOP.

POOMF!

THERE.

SHE'S AS GOOD AS NEW.

LISTEN HERE, RUNTS!

MISKIT'S GONNA NEED A CO-PILOT AND NEITHER ME OR BOTTLE HERE CAN GET ABOARD THAT PLANE, ON ACCOUNT OF US WEIGHING TOO MUCH.

THAT MEANS ONE OF YOU MIDGETS HAS TO HELP FLY THIS THING. SO WHO'S IT GONNA BE?

NAVIN'S TOO YOUNG. I'LL DO IT.

WHAT?!

IF I'M TOO YOUNG, THEN SO ARE YOU!

BESIDES, YOU KNOW I'M BETTER THAN YOU AT STUFF LIKE THIS.

BUT YOU'RE TALKING ABOUT VIDEO GAMES. THIS IS REAL LIFE!

SO?!

EM, PLEASE. LET ME FLY THE PLANE. PLEEASE.

FINE.

REALLY?

ARE YOU JOKERS FINISHED?

120

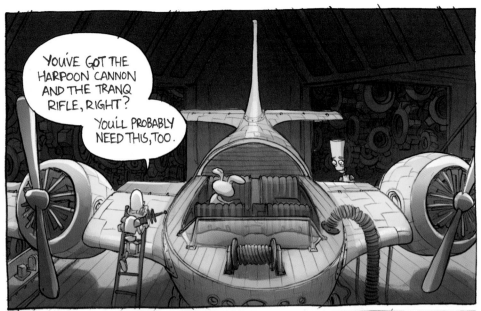

YOU'VE GOT THE HARPOON CANNON AND THE TRANQ RIFLE, RIGHT?

YOU'LL PROBABLY NEED THIS, TOO.

TO STAVE OFF THE RAKERS.

BE SWIFT.

DON'T EVEN PAUSE TO THINK.

RIGHT.

DO YOU UNDERSTAND HOW THESE CONTROLS WORK?

I THINK SO.

THEY LOOK PRETTY SIMPLE.

SPEED

YER ALL CLEAR! START HER UP!

ERR ERR ERR ERR ER

FWIP FWIP FWIP FWIP FWIP FW

VRRRRRRR...

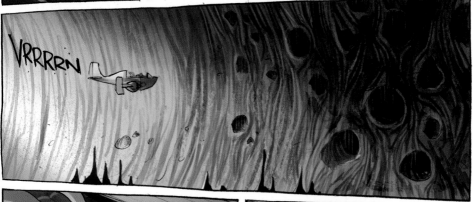

VRRRRRN

HUMMMNN

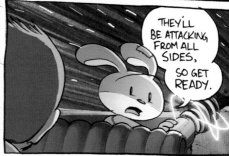

THEY'RE SO SLOW.

WE MUST BE JUST WAKING THEM UP.

IF WE MOVE QUICKLY ENOUGH, MAYBE WE WON'T HAVE TO DEAL WITH THEM.

MISKIT! BELOW US!

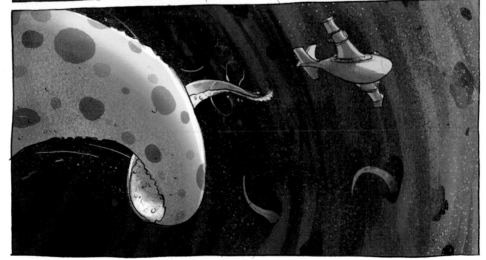

SPAK!!

GOTCHA!

ARE YOU ALL RIGHT?

I THINK SO, YES.

HEY GUYS—

IT'S GETTING CROWDED UP HERE.

131

GOOD WORK NAVIN!

CLICK! CLICK! CLICK! CLICK!

KSSSHT!

WE'RE THROUGH THE GAUNTLET!

THEY MADE IT!

HOW FAR ARE WE FROM THE ARACHNOPOD?! OVER!

THEY'RE RIGHT ON TOP OF IT!

YOU'RE RIGHT ON TOP OF IT! OVER!

HE SAYS WE'RE ABOVE IT!

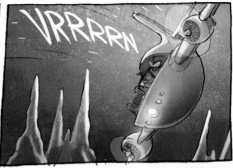
VRRRRN

I SEE IT!

THERE'S MORE THAN ONE! AND THEY'RE MOVING FAST!

NAVIN, TAKE US DOWN. BUT BE CAREFUL.

HEY LOOK!

THERE'S MOM!

I'LL GET THE TRANQ RIFLE!

KCHAK!

I HOPE THIS WORKS.

SHK!

NOW HOLD HER STEADY!

SKKNT!

THUP!

GLUG GLUG GLUG

SOMETHING'S WRONG.

IT SHOULD HAVE BEEN AFFECTED IMMEDIATELY.

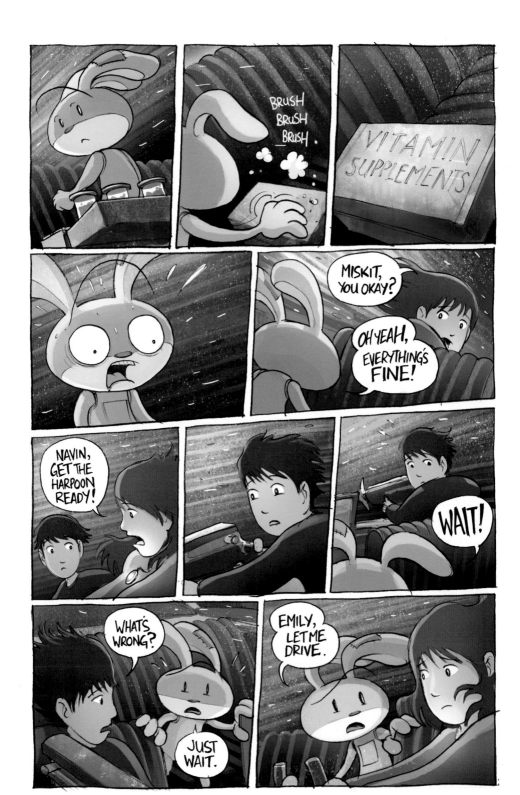

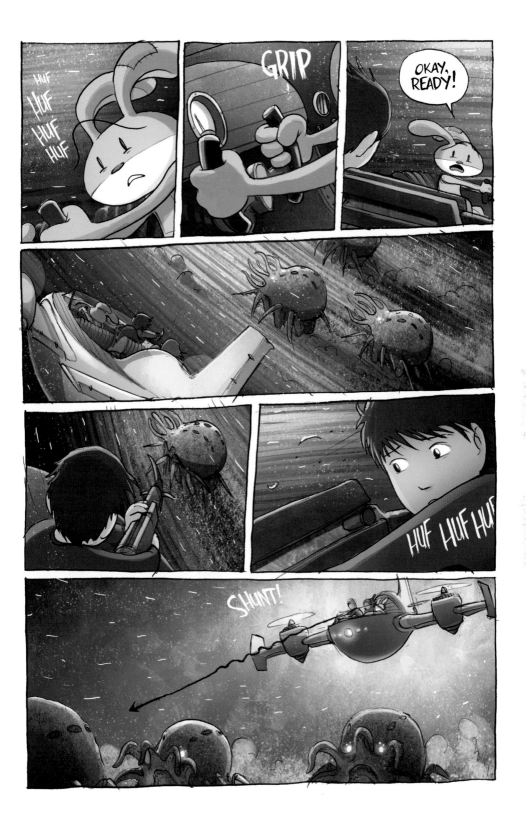

137

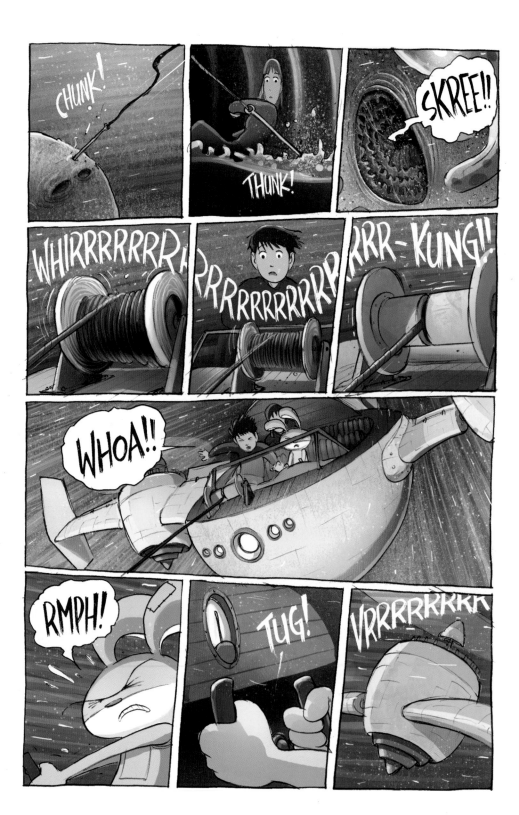

SKREE!!!

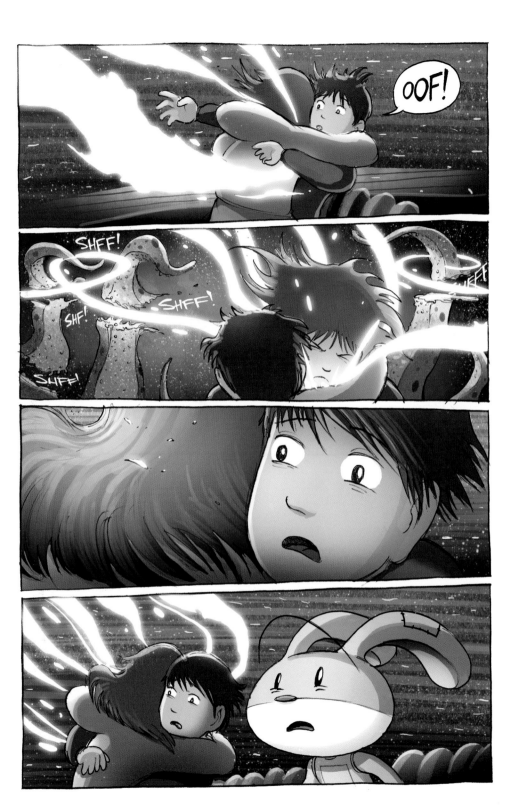

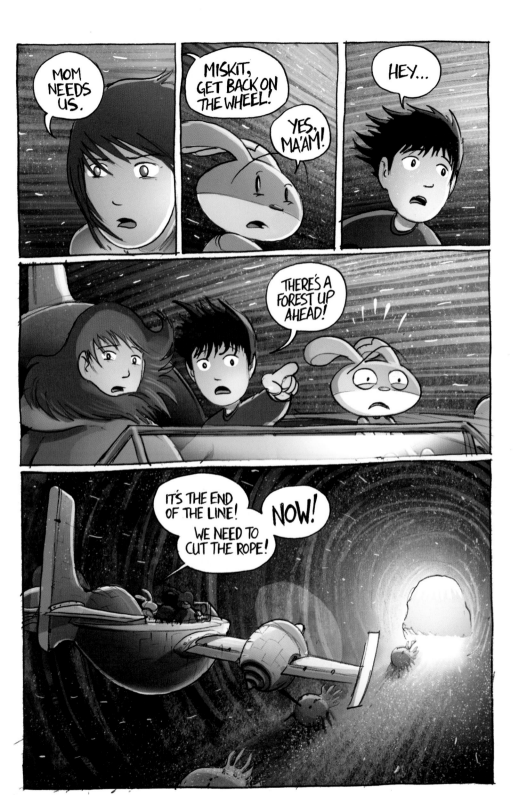

153

MISKIT?

NAVIN, STAY HERE.

EM?

EM, WAIT!

SZRAK!

SKREE!

SKREE!

SKREE!

SPLATCH!!!

UNGH!

SKSSSH!

ERGH!

IF YOU WANT THE AMULET, JUST TAKE IT! BUT LEAVE ME AND MY MOM ALONE!

WHAT MAKES YOU BELIEVE I'M AFTER THE AMULET?

IT'S NOT THE STONE I'M AFTER.

IT'S YOU.

SQUEEZE!

JUST RELAX.

ONCE HE'S INSIDE YOUR BRAIN, YOU WON'T HAVE TO THINK ANY MORE.

NO MORE WORRIES.

NO MORE FEARS.

FEAR...

NO MORE FEAR...

JUST FOCUS...

165

CHOOOM!

NO.

YOU'RE MAKING A MISTAKE, YOUNG MASTER.

RUN AWAY.

AND DON'T EVER COME NEAR ME OR MY FAMILY AGAIN. UNDERSTOOD?

Y-YES.

SPLOP!

HUF HUF

ERGH.

EM!!!

HER VITAL SIGNS ARE STABLE.

THE POISON WON'T KILL HER BUT SHE NEEDS AN ANTIDOTE.

OTHERWISE, SHE MAY NEVER WAKE UP AGAIN.

SHK!

URK!

JUST RELAX.

I PROMISED YOU WE WOULD GET HER BACK DIDN'T I?

BUT NOT LIKE THIS!

YOU DIDN'T SAY SHE WOULD BE POISONED!

HOW DO WE FIND A CURE?

DON'T WORRY, MOM.

EVERYTHING'S GOING TO BE ALL RIGHT.

RIGHT EM?

YEAH.

I THINK SO.

HEY GUYS.

IT'S TIME TO MOVE.

RUBY! THEODORE!

FURNITURE SECURED.

CHECK.

PATIENT SECURED.

CHECK.

HEY KID. HAVE A SEAT.

WE'LL BE LEAVING SHORTLY.

MISKIT, WHAT'S GOING ON?

WE NEED TO GO TO THE NEAREST CITY TO FIND AN ANTIDOTE FOR YOUR MOTHER.

AND THERE'S ONLY ONE WAY WE CAN GET THERE.

KCHUNK!

MASTERS SECURED! CHECK!

OKAY, BOTTLE.

LET'S DO THIS THING.

KDUNK!

BKOOM!

BOOSH!

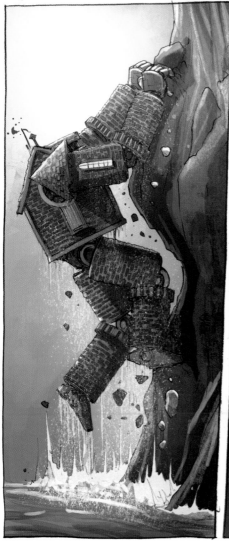

WE'RE ALMOST OUT!